Understanding
Alcohol
and Drinking
Problems

Dr Jonathan Chick

WITHDRAWN

Published by Family Doctor Publications Limited
in association with the British Medical Association

© Family Doctor Publications 1997–2009
Updated 1999, 2000, 2002, 2003, 2004, 2006, 2009

Family Doctor Publications, PO Box 4664, Poole, Dorset BH15 1NN

ISBN-13: 978-1-903474-28-0
ISBN-10: 1-903474-28-0

Contents

About the author

Dr Jonathan Chick is a consultant psychiatrist at the Alcohol Problems Clinic, Royal Edinburgh Hospital. His practice and research into the early recognition and treatment of problem drinking are acknowledged worldwide. Dr Chick has advised government departments in the USA, Canada, Australia and Britain.

Introduction

Case history: Mr Roberts

Mr Roberts was finding work increasingly difficult and dreaded the tension he felt in the mornings. He had enjoyed a drink after work for years, but now his wife and children were complaining about his irritability and asking why he was no longer the reliable husband and father they knew.

When his doctor checked his blood pressure he also asked him about his drinking. An explanation of how alcohol could actually cause tension did not make sense to him at first, but he agreed to have three weeks free of alcohol – and he felt much better.

He decided to cut drinking out of his life. With his family's support and advice from his GP, he found this much easier than he had feared, and was soon back to his former vigour and enthusiasm for family life and work.

Is too much alcohol a common problem?

Out of the UK population of 60 million people, 36 million of us are regular drinkers. Two million are heavy drinkers, and there are a million men and women in Britain who have, or have had, a serious drinking problem.

Of those, 200,000 are dependent on alcohol each day of their lives. More women are now drinking than ever before in this century. Although alcohol-related problems used to affect far more men than women, women now seek counselling for drinking problems as frequently as men.

This book explains how alcohol can have a variety of harmful as well as pleasant effects. It gives guidance on how to change a drinking pattern and succeed – whether by cutting down or abstaining completely.

Out of the UK population of 60 million people, 36 million of us are regular drinkers.

KEY POINTS

- In the UK 36 million people are regular drinkers

- Women seek counselling for drinking problems as frequently as men

What determines our drinking habits?

What is alcohol?

Beer, wine, spirits, cider, and the scores of other drinks fermented or distilled around the world, all contain ethanol. Ethanol, which belongs to a group of chemical substances called alcohols, is produced when yeast assists the fermentation of sugar to form ethanol and carbon dioxide.

How much ethanol is in alcoholic drinks?

The amount of ethanol produced is controlled either by the quantity of sugar added or by the ethanol level reaching 14 per cent by volume, after which the yeast cannot survive. The carbon dioxide produced forms the 'head' on a glass of beer and the bubbles in champagne.

The process of distillation – boiling off and concentrating the ethanol part of the beverage – was discovered in the Middle East in AD 800 by a man called Jahir ibn Hayyan. Distillation allows more concentrated and potent alcoholic drinks to be produced.

What else is in alcoholic drinks?

Other constituents (sometimes called congeners) in alcoholic drinks contribute to the taste that we may enjoy, but can also cause headache and a hangover if we have drunk a lot. The amount of congener varies – drinks with a dark colour such as red wine or brandy contain more congeners, and so cause more of a hangover than pale drinks.

How does alcohol affect us?

Although other constituents give drinks their colour, taste and character, it is ethanol that causes a change in our brain. This change can, if the circumstances are right, lead us to feel merry and talkative, or relaxed and sleepy. It is ethanol that helps us let our hair down.

Celebrating, marking special events and meeting up with friends have become occasions for drinking. The advertising and marketing of the drinks industry are designed to make sure that we continue to believe in the good things about alcohol.

Ethanol also causes some of the unpleasant effects of being intoxicated – such as the slowing of our thinking and our reactions, irritability and the tendency to do things on the spur of the moment which may be regretted later.

What are common measurements of alcohol?
Units

Many people nowadays talk in terms of 'units' of alcohol, to measure the amount. A pub measure of spirits (25 millilitres) counts as one unit. A 275 ml bottle of an Alcopop contains one and a half units.

What is a unit of alcohol?

A unit of alcohol is a handy measure and can be used to estimate the amount of alcohol that we drink. As a guide, the drinks shown below contain about one unit, but this varies depending on the strength of alcohol in the drink and the size of the glass.

| A small glass of sherry or fortified wine | A small glass of wine (125 ml) | ½ pint of beer or cider ¼ pint of strong lager | A single measure of aperitif or spirit |

A one-litre bottle of spirits – brandy, whisky or gin – contains about 40 units of alcohol

Percentage of alcohol by volume

The strength of a drink is measured as the alcohol content as a percentage, or percentage by volume (%v/v), for example, spirits 40%v/v, beer 3–5%v/v, Alcopops 5%v/v.

How is the strength of an alcoholic drink measured?

The strength of a drink is measured as the alcohol content as a percentage of the volume. This is expressed as percentage by volume or %v/v. The pie charts show the usual alcohol content found in some commonly drunk alcoholic drinks.

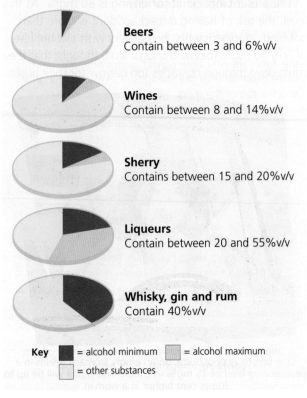

Beers
Contain between 3 and 6%v/v

Wines
Contain between 8 and 14%v/v

Sherry
Contains between 15 and 20%v/v

Liqueurs
Contain between 20 and 55%v/v

Whisky, gin and rum
Contain 40%v/v

Key   ■ = alcohol minimum   ▨ = alcohol maximum
        □ = other substances

Amount of alcohol in blood

For the purposes of measuring alcohol concentration in blood, we use the amount of alcohol (in milligrams) found in 100 millilitres of blood. This is written as 'mg per 100 ml blood' or 'mg%'.

How does alcohol affect us?

As a very rough guide, one unit of alcohol drunk on an empty stomach results in a peak alcohol level of 15 mg% in a man. This figure will be up to 30 per cent higher in a woman, for reasons that we explain later.

The present legal limit for driving is 80 mg%. At this level, the risk of having a road accident is more than doubled. In experiments, bus drivers with alcohol levels of only 50 mg% (below the legal limit) thought that they could drive through obstacles too narrow for their buses.

One unit of alcohol drunk on an empty stomach results in a peak alcohol level of 15 mg% in a man. This figure will be up to 30 per cent higher in a woman.

Concentrations of 400 mg% could block the brain's breathing control centre and be fatal, especially if sedative drugs have been taken as well.

Breath tests

In breath tests, the units used are micrograms (µg) per 100 ml of breath. The breathalyser measures the alcohol contained in each 100 ml of breath. The present legal limit for driving is 35 µg per 100 ml breath (0.35 mg per litre).

On average, the body removes alcohol from the blood at about 15 mg% per hour (that is, about one unit of alcohol is cleared per hour). This means that a person who drinks eight pints one night may still be over the legal limit driving to work the next day.

Are we drinking more than we used to?

Compared with 100 years ago, the British are probably drinking less. Gin and beer used to be cheap, and we were great importers of brandy and wine.

In 1914 Lloyd George, the British Prime Minister, was worried about the effect of alcohol on the industrial effort needed for the war, so steps were taken to reduce sales. Consumption fell dramatically and remained low in the depression years between the wars.

Consumption began to increase in 1950, however, as prosperity in Britain returned. Tax on alcoholic drinks had limited drinking, but consumption has increased since 1950, as the tax imposed became a smaller proportion of people's wages.

In real terms, alcohol became cheaper. From 1965 to 2000, the amount that each adult was drinking, on average, doubled.

Reported drinking in the UK

The two graphs show the differences in drinking patterns between women and men in the UK. The left-hand graph shows women and the right-hand graph shows men.

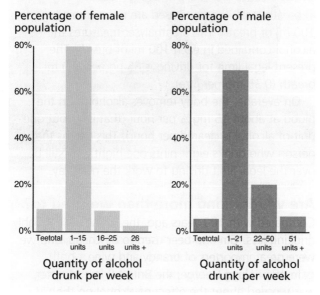

Percentage of female population

Quantity of alcohol drunk per week (Teetotal, 1–15 units, 16–25 units, 26 units +)

Percentage of male population

Quantity of alcohol drunk per week (Teetotal, 1–21 units, 22–50 units, 51 units +)

Today, drinking problems are increasing. The UK death rate for alcoholic liver disease more than doubled from 1990 to 2007.

Young people in Britain have increased the amount that they drink in a session. Young Danes are the drinkers in Europe who most often drink to get drunk.

What affects individual drinking habits?
Genetics
Some people dislike the taste or the effect of alcohol. Others like the effect from the start. This reflects their personality and their genes.

Young people in Britain have increased the amount that they drink in a session.

Drinking problems run in families. This is partly because a child who grows up with one or both parents drinking heavily may learn to do the same.

However, there is also a genetic factor. If a child whose birth mother or father had a drinking problem is adopted or fostered, he or she is more likely to have a drink problem in adulthood than his or her adopted or fostered siblings.

Identical twins, who share an identical chemical blueprint, tend to drink in a similar way because differences between people's liking for alcohol result partly from differences in body and brain chemistry. In pairs of twins where one has a drinking problem, the other twin is more likely to have a drinking problem if they are an identical pair (exactly the same genes) rather than a non-identical pair (the genes are only as alike as those of other brothers and sisters).

There is a genetic factor involved not only in whether or not people enjoy the effects of alcohol, but also in whether or not alcohol causes problems or addiction.

Social factors

Our pattern of drinking tends to be similar to that of our friends. For many people their circle of friends develops in their teenage years and changes little. People like to drink for the sociability and humour that go with it, and because it helps them break their routine. Second to watching TV, going for a drink is Britain's favourite leisure activity.

People like to drink for the sociability and humour that go with it, and because it helps them break their routine.

A new job or getting married can alter an established pattern. Spouses can have an influence on their partners' drinking. For instance, when two sisters who are identical twins stay unmarried, they are likely to go through adult life drinking in a similar pattern, whereas if one or both marry, their drinking patterns begin to differ.

In their later years, most people drink less than they did when they were 18 to 25.

Case history: Janet

Moira and Janet are identical twins who have enjoyed a close relationship ever since they were born.

After graduating from the same university they even lived together when they both got office jobs in the centre of London.

Although they chose the same career it was at different companies.

Janet's manager was an extrovert and also a keen golfer who loved the club life.

At first Janet was resentful when his bachelor lifestyle continued after they were married, but she joined in with him rather than try to change him.

Janet had not liked alcohol as a teenager and Moira became distressed as her sister gradually extended her pattern of drinking to become someone who, it seemed to Moira, always had a drink in her hand.

Work patterns

A person's job influences his or her drinking. Jobs with high exposure to alcohol include the building industry, the drinks trade, hotels and restaurants, and work that takes people away from home – such as the armed services and sales travelling.

Religious beliefs

Some faiths recommend strict moderation or even total abstinence and the faithful adhere to this. There are religious writings going back thousands of years about the problems that alcohol can cause.

Some religions give a specific place to alcohol, such as wine in Jewish family ceremonies. Occasionally members of strict communities such as Moslem societies may drink but risk disapproval. They may run into difficulties controlling their intake because they have not learned moderate drinking in their family.

Those who practise a religion are able to meet friends and take part in social gatherings without alcohol. This is in contrast to most social occasions and even some sporting events in our society, which usually involve drinking.

Drinking 'to cope'

Alcohol is our favourite drug. Occasionally people drink more because they feel that it helps them cope with a problem or blots it out.

However, one problem can become two, as the individual gets into the vicious circle called dependence, and the drinking escalates (see page 63). Dependence on alcohol can be a major problem, because drinkers begin to be unable to control how much or how often they drink, and find it very difficult to change. We explain this later.

KEY POINTS

■ How much we drink depends partly on the genes that we inherit from our parents

■ Some occupations lead to heavy drinking

■ Drinking to solve a problem can lead to two problems

Alcohol and health

How the body handles alcohol

Alcohol is absorbed from the stomach and small intestine into the bloodstream. The rate at which it is absorbed varies; it is most rapid on an empty stomach, so that a high peak level is quickly reached, and the person feels drunk quickly.

What affects the absorption of alcohol?

Food in the stomach slows down its absorption by up to 50 per cent, thus reducing the peak blood alcohol level. This also means that the same amount of alcohol stays longer in the body when the stomach is full than if it is empty.

The alcohol from wine and sherry reaches the bloodstream more quickly than that from beer, because it is more concentrated. Sugar in sweet drinks retards absorption, whereas the bubbles of carbon dioxide in champagne or gin and tonic accelerate it.

What parts of the body hold alcohol?

Alcohol is distributed throughout the body so that most tissues – the heart, brain and muscles – get the same concentration as present in the blood. The liver receives a higher concentration. Little alcohol enters fat, which has a poor blood supply.

Do women deal differently with alcohol?

Women have more of their body weight as fat and less as muscles and blood. This explains why a woman of the same weight as a man who has drunk the same amount of alcohol will have a higher level of alcohol in blood and tissue.

Women also break down less alcohol in the stomach than men. Women are therefore generally able to tolerate less alcohol than men. In pregnant women alcohol crosses the placenta into the fetus.

How does the body get rid of alcohol?

Alcohol is metabolised by the liver first to a substance called acetaldehyde which is very toxic. It is thought that acetaldehyde may be responsible for some of the physical damage caused by alcohol. Acetaldehyde is quickly changed to a non-toxic substance called acetate.

The chemical processes in the liver are complex and require many enzymes, which are substances that assist chemical processes.

The way that the liver deals with alcohol can be accelerated or retarded by medications that affect the enzymes. It also varies according to the amount of alcohol drunk, the amount that is normally drunk (what the enzymes are used to dealing with) and whether the liver is healthy or not.

Too much alcohol is toxic to the liver, and the process of handling alcohol can be slowed when the liver is diseased, as in cirrhosis of the liver, which occurs after long-term alcohol abuse (see 'Harm from heavy drinking' on page 24).

Only two to five per cent of alcohol is excreted without processing, either in the urine or in the breath.

How the body handles alcohol

Alcohol is absorbed from a drink in the stomach and travels round the body in the blood.

Alcohol is consumed in a drink

Stomach

Alcohol is absorbed into the bloodstream in the stomach and small intestine

Small intestine

Alcohol travels around the body in the bloodstream and enters organs with a rich blood supply, including:

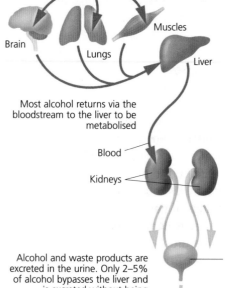

Brain

Lungs

Muscles

Liver

Most alcohol returns via the bloodstream to the liver to be metabolised

In the liver, alcohol is broken down by a chemical reaction. Waste from this process is transported in the blood to the kidneys to be excreted in the urine

Blood

Kidneys

Bladder

Alcohol and waste products are excreted in the urine. Only 2–5% of alcohol bypasses the liver and is excreted without being metabolised

Urine

Although breath concentrations are low, they reflect accurately the blood alcohol level, and this forms the basis of the breathalyser test.

Why can some people 'hold their drink' better than others?

The amount of alcohol that people can tolerate depends on a variety of factors including whether food is taken as well.

Body size

As explained earlier, women may get a higher alcohol level in the blood than men, after drinking the same amount. The bigger a person is, the more he or she can drink without appearing intoxicated.

Tolerance

The liver enzymes of a person with a regular drinking habit also become more efficient at handling alcohol, and so people who are used to alcohol can burn it off slightly quicker than first-time drinkers. Children are therefore very susceptible, being smaller in size than adults, and less experienced drinkers.

It is mainly the adjustments that the brain cells make that allow regular drinkers to drink without initially showing much effect. This tolerance of the brain cells may be the beginnings of dependence on alcohol.

Tolerance fades: heavy drinkers who abstain for a few weeks rapidly get drunk if they resume their former drinking pattern.

What are the effects of alcohol on the body?

Heart and blood circulation

Alcohol causes an increase in heart rate, and dilates the skin blood vessels, producing a flush. The flush is severe in some people of Chinese or Japanese origin.

This causes a feeling of warmth, although body temperature may actually fall because heat from the body is lost through the skin. Drinking brandy from the neck cask of a St Bernard dog who has rescued you in snow could lead to hypothermia!

Abdominal organs

Alcohol stimulates the release of gastric acids, and can lead to inflammation of the stomach lining. Alcohol also has a diuretic effect, causing more urine to be produced.

Brain

However, most people drink for the effects of alcohol on the brain. At blood levels of about 50 mg% most people feel relaxed and carefree.

At higher concentrations more brain functions are affected. Speech becomes slurred, memory is impaired and the eyes focus with difficulty.

At 100 mg% movement starts to become careless and clumsy, and emotional control and judgement may be impaired. Alcohol can cause people to take more risks.

At 200–300 mg% most people are very drunk, and may become unconscious. The level at which alcohol becomes fatal varies – what a hard drinking man regularly tolerates may kill a young girl who has never had a drink before.

After the level of alcohol in the blood has peaked, there is a phase when the individual may feel tired, depressed and irritable.

What are the immediate effects of alcohol on the body?

Women may get a higher blood alcohol level than men after drinking the same amount and, in general, the bigger a person the less potent the same amount of alcohol will be. The following are the immediate effects of alcohol:

- Increases the heart rate
- Dilates blood vessels in the skin
- Stimulates the release of gastric juices
- High doses irritate the stomach lining
- May have a diuretic effect – more urine is produced
- Speech may become slurred
- Memory is impaired
- Eyes focus with difficulty
- Movement and coordination may be impaired
- Affects emotional control and judgement
- High doses cause unconsciousness which puts people at grave risk of choking
- High doses may block the breathing centre in the brain

What causes a hangover?

The effects of the congeners in drinks cause the nausea, headache, tremulousness and tiredness that we recognise as a hangover. Dehydration may contribute, and drinking alcohol with sufficient water may prevent some symptoms.

However, as blood levels of alcohol fall during the night, there is a rebound wakefulness, and some of the heightened sensitivity and restlessness is caused by withdrawal. Contrary to popular myth, mixing drinks

The effects of the congeners in drinks cause the nausea, headache, tremulousness and tiredness that we recognise as a hangover.

does not cause a hangover, and nor does avoiding mixing prevent one! It is more likely that, if you do mix drinks, you are taking a large dose of alcohol, which gives you more of a headache the next day.

Harm from heavy drinking
The immediate problems

A large enough dose of alcohol can kill by blocking the breathing centre in the brain. Even if the amount taken is not directly fatal, the deep unconsciousness that it causes puts people at risk of dying from exposure, or choking and suffocating on their own vomit.

Harm from alcohol

Estimates of the involvement of drinking in accidents and crime show that it is a common cause of harm. Alcohol consumption is implicated in:

- 80% of deaths from fires
- 65% of serious head injuries
- 50% of murders
- 40% of road traffic accidents
- 30% of accidents in the home

Other short-term problems include dehydration and low blood sugar, which can be dangerous for young and elderly people, and people taking treatment for diabetes.

Accidents

The most common reason for drinkers seeing a doctor is an injury caused by drunkenness. When people are drunk they are a danger to themselves and to others. Alcohol is associated with the accidents shown in the box above.

Alcohol consumption is implicated in 80 per cent of deaths from fires.

Alcohol is a factor in road, rail, shipping and airplane accidents. One-third of private pilots killed have alcohol in their blood.

The accident rate for heavy drinkers at work is three times the normal. About 60 per cent of fatal accidents at work are alcohol related.

For more information on drinking and driving, see page 100.

Alcohol also leads to greater risk-taking, and may lead to a person making him- or herself vulnerable to crime and assault, both physical and sexual.

The longer-term problems of heavy drinking

Heavy drinking means more than five units per day for women or seven units per day for men. Safe limits are up to a maximum of three units per day for women and four units per day for men.

Even so, the Chief Medical Officer has recommended that drinking one to two units a day confers the best health benefits without risk, and that regularly drinking up to a maximum safe limit can lead to problems. And the more the safe limit is exceeded, the more likely illness becomes.

Heart and circulation

From the age of 40, when coronary heart disease begins to affect susceptible people, one to three units a day may help prevent heart attacks and angina.

Another type of heart disease occurs in people drinking over 10 units per day. It results from damage to the heart muscle and causes breathlessness and palpitations (a fluttering feeling in the heart), swelling of the ankles and accumulation of fluid in the lungs. Alcohol can cause strokes, partly as a result of high blood pressure, so people with high blood pressure should cut down their drinking.

Digestive system

The irritation to your stomach lining caused by alcohol can cause loss of appetite. When severe, it results in pain, vomiting and bleeding.

The pancreas lies behind your stomach and is also sensitive to alcohol. When its cells become inflamed the pain is very severe. If it becomes damaged permanently, your pancreas cannot make enough

The irritation to your stomach lining caused by alcohol can cause loss of appetite. When severe, it results in pain, vomiting and bleeding.

insulin, causing diabetes. Enzymes that break food down are not produced and diarrhoea and malnutrition can result.

Liver

Liver problems can be deceptive. Although a blood test from your family doctor could show that alcohol is causing harm to your liver, you may notice nothing for years. By then it can be too late.

Alcohol can cause several problems with the liver. At first they are mild but as drinking continues they become more serious:

- Fat deposits cause mild symptoms
- Hepatitis and jaundice are more serious
- Cirrhosis can be life threatening.

In mild cases, fat gets deposited in the liver, causing the cells to bulge. The liver increases in size, giving rise to vague abdominal discomfort and nausea.

In more serious cases, alcoholic hepatitis occurs. Here, the liver cells are inflamed and damaged. The person may feel well, but more often feels ill and weak, and may be jaundiced.

Jaundice is a yellowing of the skin caused by the accumulation, in the blood, of a substance called bilirubin, which is then deposited in the skin. One of the liver's roles is to process bilirubin to keep the level steady, but, when it is diseased, this process breaks down and the level of bilirubin starts to climb.

In the final stage of alcohol damage, cirrhosis occurs. Here, the alcohol has caused permanent damage. The cells of the liver are destroyed, and scarring occurs. The liver's function is compromised. Proteins needed to maintain muscle are not produced.

A person with cirrhosis is often, but not always, jaundiced. Water swells the abdomen ('ascites') and the feet and legs ('oedema').

The scarring and distortion block the flow of blood into the liver. The back pressure that this causes leads to varicose veins swelling up in the stomach and gullet – and these can bleed and bleed.

Cirrhosis is eventually life threatening. The only cure is liver transplantation. As a result of the shortage of donor organs, doctors may be unwilling to recommend someone who has abused alcohol for this treatment, unless an undertaking to stop drinking is agreed.

If cirrhosis has not reached the life-threatening stage, stopping drinking will often halt further damage and allow a reasonable quality of life. People who have hepatitis C virus are advised to stop drinking, to reduce the risk of cirrhosis.

Cancer
Alcohol can cause cancer in the mouth, throat and gullet. Smoking contributes to these too. Breast cancer is more likely in women who drink more than two units per day.

Brain and nerves
Some heavy drinkers lose mental faculties, especially the ability to remember new things and recent events. It is an exaggeration of what happens in old age.

Others damage their balance mechanism or get pins and needles in the feet and hands; combined with alcohol-induced loss of muscle, this leads to great difficulty in walking.

People who drink sometimes do not take a balanced diet and this can result in vitamin deficiency. Alcohol reduces the body's ability to absorb vitamins from food and a deficiency of vitamin B$_1$ (thiamine) is linked to nerve and brain damage in heavy drinkers.

Blood

Alcohol causes changes in the blood cells. Your doctor may unexpectedly find an abnormal test result, due to alcohol, when your blood is taken for some other reason.

Regular drinkers may have enlarged red blood cells, but this itself is not dangerous. However, a lack of platelets in the blood may lead to bleeding in the stomach or brain.

Blood tests to check how the liver is functioning may show an abnormal result long before liver disease develops. Your doctor will explain whether a result

Your doctor may suggest that you have a blood test to assess how well your body is coping with excessive drinking.

indicates serious illness. Gamma-glutamyl transferase (GGT) measurement is the liver test that has the most sensitivity to drinking.

If you are planning to reduce your alcohol intake, you can ask your doctor to monitor the tests. This gives you and your doctor a way of measuring whether you are being successful in cutting down!

There is now a new blood test called carbohydrate-deficient transferase (CDT) which is more accurate than older tests in showing excessive drinking and changes in drinking.

Mental illness

Alcohol can cause mental illness. It alters the brain chemistry to cause depressed mood. This can, of course, also harm important relationships with friends and family.

It may be believed, wrongly, that a partner is having an affair and drinking can cause the situation to be blown up out of all proportion.

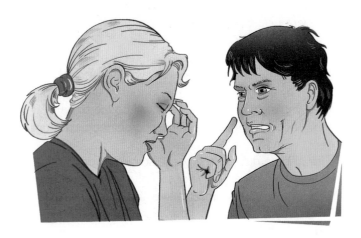

Excess alcohol consumption can cause relationship problems.

Fortunately quite rare, there is another illness in which the brain can be so damaged that hallucinations occur which may go on for weeks or months. The 'voices' may say threatening or derogatory things that are frightening. This can nearly always be cured by medical treatment and avoiding all alcohol.

Your complexion

Regular heavy drinkers give their habit away by their red and blotchy faces, with tiny extra blood vessels in the cheeks and eyes. The bulging red nose comes only after 15 years of tippling!

Some people have a condition called psoriasis in which the skin develops red patches and the surface layer is white and flaky. It comes and goes – and heavy drinking can bring on an episode.

Your weight

Alcoholic drinks are calories without vitamins. A glass of wine or half a pint of lager contains about the same number of calories as a thick slice of bread and butter. Therefore drinkers can put on weight.

The beer belly is well named – three pints of beer a day or twenty-one pints per week will increase your weight by about two kilograms in four weeks. Two or three single gin and tonics a day will do the same. And, of course, the same will happen in the next four weeks – and so on!

Drinking a glass of sherry can stimulate your appetite, but drinking five or six units regularly without food irritates your stomach lining and causes nausea. This is why some drinkers lose weight and feel weak and easily tired.

Benefits to health

The news on alcohol is not all bad. Used in moderation, some people will actually have better health.

Social well-being

Introducing a 'cocktail hour' in old people's homes improves mobility, memory and social interaction. Requests for sleeping tablets can go down. Small amounts of alcohol can make life seem a little more colourful.

Heart disease

Medical research has found that people who drink moderately – one to three units a day – have less chance than abstainers of getting heart disease. This beneficial effect is seen most in people over the age of 40, and when the alcoholic drink is taken at mealtimes.

Alcohol helps to prevent blood clots forming in the arteries. As heart disease is a common cause of death in western society, it means that light/moderate drinkers have a longer life expectancy than either abstainers or heavy drinkers. We can, of course, reduce the chance that we will get heart disease in other ways – stopping smoking, losing weight, eating less animal fats and more fruit and vegetables, and taking more exercise.

Getting a job where we feel in control and achieve satisfaction helps too. People whose pattern is to drink one to three units per day tend to be in that category and often also have a sensible diet – this may contribute to why they have better health. Governments do not advise people to drink to protect their health – if we were told that one or two drinks were good for us, we could imagine that three or four would be even better!

Bones

In middle age and later, women who drink a little have stronger bones than those who are teetotal. Heavy drinking, however, can make bones thinner and may lead to more fractures. The advice, as always, is moderation.

Sex

Does alcohol improve sex? For some people, a drink can increase their desire. If tension is impeding their enjoyment of sex then relaxing with alcohol can help.

Large doses of alcohol block the nerves necessary for sexual function, however, which in the man raises the fear of impotence. If this happens more than once

Large doses of alcohol block the nerves necessary for sexual function.

or twice he may get seriously worried about his sexual ability – and worrying about performance is a sure way to impair erection, until confidence is re-established with a sympathetic partner.

Is there a safe limit?

For a woman, the chance of having liver disease or breast cancer begins to go up once she is drinking three units per day. Some people have more resistant bodies than others but we have no way yet of telling in advance who they are.

A man's liver can stand slightly more, but regular drinking of five units per day (35 per week) has been shown to be the start of problems for some men. The safe limit for regular drinking is two units per day for women, three units per day for men.

People who drink in occasional sessions should stick to fewer than eight units (five for women) to avoid the dangers associated with being drunk. The media today commonly talk about 'binge drinking'.

Pregnancy

Alcohol can damage genes, leading to abnormal development in the fetus. Most pregnancies with abnormal fetuses miscarry – and pregnant women who drink heavily have twice the rate of miscarriage compared with non-drinkers.

If a woman drinks heavily during pregnancy, she runs the risk of having a baby with 'fetal alcohol syndrome', in which the baby is mentally handicapped with abnormal facial features, and a variety of neurological, heart, bone and kidney defects.

Pregnant women should abstain from alcohol, or at the very least restrict alcohol intake to the occasional

Pregnant women should abstain from alcohol, or at the very least restrict alcohol intake to the occasional drink.

drink. Early in pregnancy is the time of greatest danger.

Alcohol appears in breast milk in breast-feeding mothers, but the occasional drink before breast-feeding will do no harm.

Alcohol and prescribed drugs

The effect of alcohol on prescribed drugs depends on the drug, and on whether alcohol is taken in a one-off binge, or as part of a chronic problem.

In the first instance, alcohol competes with the drug for liver enzymes, and so the drug is broken down

It can be dangerous to drink alcohol if you are taking these medications

- Benzodiazepine tranquillisers, e.g. lorazepam, diazepam (Valium)
- Other tranquillisers, e.g. olanzapine (Zyprexa), risperidone (Risperdal), sulpiride, chlorpromazine
- Many antidepressants, e.g. dothiepin (dosulepin or Prothiaden), amitriptyline, mirtazapine, trazodone (Molipaxin), clomipramine (Anafranil)
- Sleeping tablets
- Most antihistamines
- Antiepileptic drugs, e.g. phenytoin (Epanutin), phenobarbital
- Warfarin

more slowly and becomes 'stronger', and works for longer. This can be dangerous, because it is effectively an overdose. The drugs in this category include those in the box.

The most common danger of taking alcohol while on a medication comes with any drug that has a sedative effect, however slight. The sedative effect of the alcoholic drink may double the sedative effect of the drug, resulting in accidents. Sedatives include tranquillisers, many antidepressants, antihistamines and all sleeping tablets.

When drinking is heavy and prolonged, the effect is to speed up the liver enzymes (as they get used to dealing with a big load), and so some drugs get dealt with more quickly than normal, and thus have a lesser effect than normal. Drug dosage may need to be

Alcohol can reduce the effect of some medications

When drinking is heavy and regular, the liver becomes accustomed to working harder to process the extra alcohol. Medication taken may be processed faster and so have a lesser effect. This can happen with the following:

- Drugs for epilepsy
- Some antibiotics
- Some drugs to lower blood pressure
- Some antidepressants

increased by the doctor. The drugs in this category include those in the box above.

Some drugs will interact with alcohol to produce an unpleasant flushing, for example, the anti-diabetic medication chlorpropamide and the antimicrobial metronidazole (Flagyl).

KEY POINTS

- Drinking on an empty stomach means that alcohol reaches the brain in a burst

- Drinking one to three units per day can reduce the chance of heart disease; more than that can harm health

- One unit has the same calories as a slice of bread and butter

- Alcohol is a factor in some types of cancer

Effects of drinking on daily life

Drinking in the family

Having a drink on a special occasion is part of our culture. If families do this together and include teenagers, without people getting drunk, it helps the younger members learn to handle alcohol safely.

A complete ban on alcohol can lead a teenager to rebel by drinking, to be different from the family – with all the risks that such behaviour involves.

When someone in the family drinks too much

Drinking can lead to changes in the way we react to people, which can damage relationships very badly.

A father becomes inconsistent with his children – and loses patience with them. He may lose their respect. They may respond by rebelling or retreating into their shells.

He is less sensitive to his wife's needs and wishes. He is not much company in the evenings if he has been drinking and is now often asleep in a chair. If she complains, he becomes defensive.

Temper is less controlled and angry outbursts may become common.

Case history: Simon

Simon had worked hard, step by step, up the Civil Service ladder. As new work practices were introduced, he found himself more and more often drinking after work and collapsing as soon as he arrived home.

His wife resented making a meal that he sometimes never touched. When he stirred himself in time for the BBC news, he barked at the children. They had been used to a father who was always ready to help with homework or fit for a game of football before supper. His wife told him what was happening, but he seemed to ignore it. She begged him to get some help but he said that she was exaggerating and blamed his bosses.

He was stunned and very distressed, when he returned from a two-day meeting in London, to find that she had left with the two children. She had gone to live in a flat that she had rented, leaving only her sister's address through which all messages would henceforth be communicated.

If a mother is drinking too much, the same can happen. She does not cope so well with family responsibilities and so her husband may take control. That may make her angry.

The children get used to not taking notice of what she says because when she has been drinking she exaggerates or does not make much sense.

Case history: Mary

'Get out of here and find yourself somewhere to live – somewhere selfish people like you can learn the hard way,' Mary screamed. Tina slammed the door, a bit harder than the last time they argued.

Her sports bag was already packed together with her railcard and the phone number of her friend from year 11 at school. She knew that her mother could be like this if she'd been drinking all evening, but nowadays it was happening most days.

Next morning, Mary would wake in a panic, remembering in a haze her row with her daughter, feeling sick with guilt. Why could she not talk to her any longer, why was it rows always, why was a responsible mother losing hold of her life?

It took Mary another two years to win back Tina's affection and respect, and in that time Mary had to face something that she had hedged around for at least two years before that – a bad-tempered, hurt and critical side of her came out whenever she drank and she seemed no longer able to control her drinking.

Alcohol can be a significant drain on family finances. Resentments will grow if what used to be spent on a family outing or holiday is now going on drink. Alcohol causes a shrunken bank account more often than it causes a shrunken brain, but both have serious results.

Drinking is one cause of marriages splitting up. Some partners give ample warning of their intention to leave and the drinker may hear and take action. At other times the message is not heard or does not get through. Sometimes a spouse leaves knowing that the relationship has changed but is not clear enough about the cause to make a specific complaint.

When mother or father is drinking in a way that affects the family, it may cause embarrassment. Friends are no longer invited to the house. The drinking problem is kept a secret, as if it was a slur on the family.

Alcohol problems can run in families

We explain why alcohol problems can run in families on pages 11–12. If mother, father or another close relative has a drink problem, then the next generation should be advised to take great care in using alcohol.

Drinking to cope with stress

You've all heard someone say, 'Drinking helps me cope' or 'Alcohol is a solution to my problems, not a problem itself' or 'I need a drink to wind down'.

Alcohol is a sedative, and if your mind or body is tense alcohol will combat that. If the dose is big enough, alcohol induces sleep.

Research shows, however, that regular drinking to relieve tension can do the opposite. If your nervous system gets used to alcohol, it is as if your nerve cells call out for the next dose. For example, if we regularly take a nightcap to get to sleep, we may find we have difficulty getting off to sleep without one.

Case history: Andrew

Andrew is a salesman who gets tense at work, because of difficult customers and the targets his boss sets him.

If he takes a drink at lunch time to relax, he may feel like another on the way home after work.

If he next takes a drink in the evening at home, there is some alcohol in the body almost round the clock.

Then he will begin to feel more tense and anxious than usual first thing in the morning.

He may believe this is due to the worrying thoughts he has about how to face the day, but it may actually be a result of his body chemistry 'wanting' the next drink.

Case history: John

John was a perfectionist and proud. He gave himself and his family hell whenever there was some DIY repair job in the house and he failed to get a screw to fit to the last millimetre. He'd storm out of the house to get a drink and come back drunk and even more grumpy.

When his family at last got across to him how pointless his anger was, he began to take a new attitude. He actually started to enjoy taking time to do things, instead of rushing and drinking too much alcohol.

His catch phrase became 'I'm keeping things in perspective'. He learned to live in the present moment, and to take pleasure in that, without continually letting himself feel under pressure. Living with John became much easier!

Drinking to cope with stress can be counterproductive in another way – it can be tricky to get the amount just right so that anxiety is relieved but performance is still OK. The bride's father who dreads having to make a speech at the reception is occasionally over the top!

There are other ways to deal with tension. Here are some tips that have helped many busy people.

Managing tension
Set limits on what people demand of you
We all have a right to say 'No'. It is perfectly reasonable to tell people that you have to put a stop on what, and how much, you take on.

Be easier on yourself – and others
Don't aim for perfection. You can do your best, given the circumstances. It is OK to be 'good enough'.

Accept what cannot be changed
Fight the battles that you can win, not those you cannot win. What is the point of burning up with anger about things that won't change?

Delegate!
If you cannot face the household chores after a day at work, get the family to do more. But ask them firmly and clearly, otherwise they may not know that you mean it. And make it clear that it is to be done properly.

In the workplace, people may believe that they are delegating, but check whether there is something else others could be doing to relieve you.

Check how you react to criticism
If it was correct, can you learn from it? If the criticism

How to cope when work is piling up

Sometimes you can feel overwhelmed by the sheer volume of work with which you have to deal. Taking a drink is not good medicine. It is better to be methodical and see if the following tips help:

- List jobs by priority: do the first one and clear it before starting the next
- Pace yourself: we can only get through so much
- Limit interruptions
- Check reality: 'In the past I got through a lot of work, so I'll manage this time as well'
- Papers piling up? If urgent do it; if no action needed, bin it

is not correct, remember that others have a right to their opinions. You can agree to disagree.

Too much to get done?
If you feel that you have too much to get through, and you start to think 'I can't handle this', then tension builds up. Combat this by pacing yourself and taking on one job at a time.

Drinking to help you sleep
Advantage
Alcohol is a sedative. A drink at bedtime can help people get off to sleep sooner than they might otherwise.

Disadvantages
As alcohol is burnt up by the body, its level in the blood falls – so if sleep was artificially induced by

alcohol there can be a rebound effect causing unpleasant wakefulness at 2 or 3am.

The other disadvantage of alcohol as a sleeping potion is that, if you use it regularly over two or three

Tips to help you sleep without using alcohol

Rather than use alcohol to help you sleep – with its many drawbacks – the techniques listed below have been proved to work, and are simple to use and have no disadvantages:

- Take more physical exercise
- Avoid tea, coffee and other caffeine-containing drinks such as Cola after 6pm
- Go to bed later, having found something interesting and enjoyable to do in the evening – such as read a book or newspaper, do a jigsaw or crossword puzzle or watch a video
- Have a bedtime snack – a small amount of carbohydrate and fat, such as toast and a hot milky drink, has been shown to help sleep
- Relax in a warm bath
- When you go to bed, lie still – you can rest your body without sleeping; a relaxation method can help, such as long slow breaths and letting your muscles flop loose
- Use a self-hypnosis relaxation tape
- If worries fill your head as soon as it touches the pillow, keep a piece of paper handy and write your worries down as they occur. You can tackle them in the morning when your mind is fresh – a tired mind can trick you into thinking that a problem is insoluble

weeks, your brain's sleep centre expects it and will not switch over into sleep easily without it.

Worrying about not sleeping

Some people worry when they feel that they are not getting enough sleep. They believe in a magic seven or eight hours. But the need for sleep varies greatly and many people need only four or five hours.

If people have little to keep them occupied and interested, however, they may start to worry, go to bed earlier and try to sleep more. This can be difficult because sleep cannot be willed – the brain's sleep centre has its own rhythm. Worrying about not getting to sleep is a sure way to stay awake.

If you use sleeping tablets, take care with alcohol because it adds to their effect.

Drinking to avoid 'the blues'

The first effect of alcohol – when the setting and atmosphere are right – is a feeling of well-being. But when the alcohol level in your blood falls back you tend to feel tired and out of sorts. This can lead some people to experience depressed, hopeless feelings and thoughts.

If you associate feeling well and happy with the first drink, you may use alcohol to meet a period of depression. Some people are prone to low mood, and there is an illness in which low mood and pessimism can occur out of the blue, called depressive illness.

Meeting good friends and keeping an active social life relieve depression – but taking a drink as a remedy is usually not good medicine. The way to recover is to get our thinking straight, improve our relationships with others and have a variety of interests and activities.

Case history: Granny Shaw

It was her grandchildren who first said it directly to her. 'Nanny,' as they then called her, 'Why do you always drink sherry?'

The loneliness that she had felt since her husband's long incapacity and eventual death was now worse.

GRANNY SHAW OFTEN LOOKED AFTER HER GRANDCHILDREN...

WHY DO I NEVER SEE THEM ANY MORE?

During those years, she had let her own interests flag and did not keep up with friends. Yet since he died, although she was now free of the burden of his suffering, her life had got even darker.

At first, sherry helped, but now it was a habit that she could not, and did not want to, break.

It saddened her daughter who had begun to look for a child-minder for after school. She was no longer confident that she could safely leave her children with her mother because she was now so erratic. However, that would remove her mother's only contact with other people and she could not bring herself to do so.

BUT HER SHERRY DRINKING HAD BECOME A PROBLEM...

WHY DO YOU ALWAYS DRINK SHERRY? GRANNY?

I CAN'T TRUST MUM ANY MORE. I'LL HAVE TO FIND A CHILD-MINDER WHEN I GO BACK TO WORK!

Coping with depression

Here are some points that people have found more helpful than drinking alcohol when they find that depression, or 'nervous exhaustion' as it is sometimes called, threatens to take them over.

Depression is a form of fatigue

It is as if your mental batteries are low and you need to recharge them. While the batteries are low, your brain may not be as efficient as usual, so be easy on yourself.

It passes. It may lift as suddenly as it came. Or you get better in steps, with some bad days but more and more good days.

Challenge faulty thinking

For example, one person may criticise something you did, which does not that mean you are 'totally incapable' if the reality is that most of the time you do things correctly.

Keep your perspective

If something has gone wrong take care that you are not making a catastrophe out of it. You may have made an error, but that does not write you off totally.

You are still the person you were, with your qualities and weaker spots, your experience and your skills. It cannot logically be the end of the world.

Avoid mind-reading

Do not immediately jump to a negative conclusion. Do you sometimes think, automatically, that people are thinking the worst of you? If so, you may react defensively or even aggressively to someone before they say or do anything.

Friendships or enjoyable occasions can be spoiled this way. Don't try to read minds. We cannot tell what others are thinking or feeling until they tell us.

It does not always matter what others are thinking – do what makes you feel better.

Avoid living by fixed rules

If you have excessively high expectations you set yourself up for feeling like a failure. Thinking 'I must' or 'I should' can lead to guilt or disappointment if you do not achieve all your targets.

Be easier on yourself (and others!). Be more forgiving. Say 'I would like to' or 'I prefer to' instead of the tyrannical 'musts' and 'shoulds'.

Keep an open mind

If you bring in history ('here we go again' or 'it's always like this for me') you stop yourself having new experiences and miss out on openings and chances.

Don't try to read minds. We cannot tell what others are thinking or feeling until they tell us.

Avoid black-and-white thinking

No one, including you, is totally successful or a total loser. If you hear yourself thinking any of the 'totallys', take care. Do not write someone off because he or she made a mistake. That includes you.

Look out for thinking 'poor-me'

If you find yourself thinking 'no-one knows what I'm going through', this could be wasting valuable emotional energy. It may frighten off those who would like to help you. Sometimes it can help to remind yourself that there are people worse off.

If you really have had a bad deal, try to work out how you can stop letting it get under your skin. Why give them the satisfaction of seeing you go under?

Avoid thinking 'poor me' because this will not help you solve your problems and may frighten off those people who would like to help you.

Speak up for yourself

This helps you value yourself more – and you'll find that others will too. Be open and direct, using 'I would like', 'I feel' or 'No, I do not wish to'. Speak calmly and concisely, but firmly. Repeat what you have to say if necessary, to be sure that you have been heard.

Don't use alcohol for this – people may think it's the drink talking or you may come across as aggressive. Do not insist on winning every point, just the ones that are important to you. Being aggressive may alienate others.

When you feel angry about something someone has done, you can say, 'When you do that I feel angry. This is what I would prefer you to do instead'. In this way they may see something that they did not see before.

Others will know what you want and feel only if you put it into words. Do not rely on telepathy!

Deal with loneliness

We need contact with others. The loss of a loved one or the break-up of a relationship can leave you feeling numb. But it is vital to start meeting old friends and making new ones as soon as possible.

Do not be discouraged if your first attempts come to nothing. Clubs, churches, offering your services to a voluntary organisation, attending classes are all possible. Check your local newspaper or the public library notice board.

Boredom is a serious medical condition!

There must be something out there in a world of such diversity to interest you. Learn poetry, become a bonsai expert, take a car maintenance course – anything!

Finally, your doctor can prescribe medication for depressive illness that helps gradually over a period of three to six weeks. It is important to persevere through any initial side effects that you may feel.

Antidepressant medication

Alcohol may interfere with the effect of antidepressants. If you want to have a drink, and that does not go against your doctors' instructions or any goal that you have set yourself to abstain, then take a maximum of only one drink, that is half a pint of beer or one glass of wine) if taking antidepressants, and never mix that with driving (see page 100).

KEY POINTS

- A family may try to hide the fact that someone is drinking too much

- Alcohol can disturb sleep

- Alcohol can make depression worse

- There are mental techniques for getting out of tension and depression

How to recognise a drinking problem

If the unwanted effects of drinking are harming your life in some way – your health, your relationships with those you care about, your work – then you have a drinking problem.

If you are beginning to need alcohol and find it hard to take it or leave it, or it is becoming difficult to control the amount that you drink, then you are becoming 'dependent' on alcohol and that can cause other problems to develop.

Ask yourself the following questions and be frank about the answers.

Are there changes in relationships?

The pleasant releasing effect of drinking allows you to 'let your hair down' – which can also alienate people and hurtful things can be said. After drinking, as the level of alcohol in your blood falls, you can get bad-tempered and irritable.

Drinkers can get touchy – seeing slights where none was intended. Bottled up envy or jealousy may come

Commitments may be skipped, or even forgotten

out in a destructive way. If large quantities of alcohol are drunk, the memory can be patchy for some of these moments – moments that may have been very upsetting for others.

Commitments may be skipped, or even forgotten: a father lets his son down over a promised outing to a football match; a mother loses interest in her teenage daughter's fashion pursuits.

There may be repercussions throughout the family – children become defiant, sulky or unhappy. They do less well at school. The spouse grows cold or distant, hurt by things said, and by the arguments that develop about the drinking.

Friendships are sometimes damaged in a similar way. People who drink a lot may also develop a habit of phoning friends when intoxicated, perhaps at unsociable hours, and pouring out their troubles in an insensitive way.

Are there changes in my work performance?

Frequent lateness at work or sick leave can signal that an employee is drinking too much, resulting in hangovers the next day.

Employers may overlook odd days off, but colleagues who have to bear the brunt of absences may be less patient. Drinkers often think that no-one notices extended lunch breaks (to get a drink) or the smell of alcohol on their breath.

Have I become dependent?

Has life become more oriented around places, occasions and company where there is going to be a drink? Previous hobbies or interests may get displaced in favour of drinking.

Instead of just wanting a drink the feeling is of actually needing a drink. This is due to a mixture of habit and a chemical process, to which some people may be more prone than others.

When people with this pattern of drinking try to cut down, they may find it very difficult. The thought of a drink is strongly triggered in situations where they used to drink or when they are with the same friends.

Drinkers often think that no-one notices extended lunch breaks (to get a drink) or the smell of alcohol on their breath.

How dependent have I become?
Early signs of dependence

In the early stages, our brain cells become used to alcohol, so that a rebound of sudden tension or anxiety occurs if brain cells are deprived of alcohol when the next drink is not there. This feeling may be mistaken for anxiety about going to work, worry about the family or some other connection that the person has made.

Drinkers may not readily see, or wish to see, the connection between these feelings and the fact that they have got into a very regular pattern of drinking in recent weeks or months.

Another sign of early dependence in drinkers is when they drink much more than they intend. They may say they feel that they cannot control their drinking as well as they used to – although they may have had poor control from early in their drinking days.

Previous hobbies or interests can be displaced in favour of drinking.

Friends and family may recognise the trouble, but remain helpless because people who are developing a drink problem often see things differently, because they have become attached to drinking and do not want to admit that it is time to cut back.

Alcohol dependence

A person who is dependent on alcohol has an irresistible compulsion to drink, which takes priority over almost everything else in life. There are a number of signs that this is happening and these are listed below.

Early signs of dependence

- Drinking pattern tending to be the same each day
- Setting a limit but not sticking to it
- Giving up activities that do not involve drink
- Having some problems caused by drinking but not noticing, and/or letting it happen again
- A larger amount needed to give the same effect

Later signs of dependence

- Sleep problems
- Nervous, sickly, sweaty or shaky in the morning
- Regularly having a drink within three hours of waking
- Sometimes severe withdrawal symptoms: epileptic seizures, when people suddenly lose consciousness hours or days after stopping drinking, perhaps with jerking of the arms and legs and interrupted breathing; and delirium tremens, when people become confused, not knowing where they are or whom they are with, and can have hallucinations

Later signs of dependence

When the problem goes to the next stage, the rebound feelings may be accompanied by tremor of the hands or fingers, especially in the morning when the blood alcohol level is low. A feeling of butterflies in the stomach may be there too, or nausea when the teeth are brushed or breakfast contemplated. A drink settles this – and so drinking in the morning becomes a habit.

The rebound symptoms are also called withdrawal symptoms. If someone has been drinking 16 or more units per day, for several weeks, and then stops for some reason, these can be very unpleasant.

At their severest, an epileptic fit can occur, or a temporary delirious state when the person loses touch with reality and has hallucinations (delirium tremens or 'DTs'). It is very important to avoid such a severe reaction and medication from a doctor can prevent it, if taken at the point when drinking stops.

A mysterious feature of dependence on alcohol is the ease with which the cycle of abstinence, drinking and dependence can be repeated. If a person stops drinking for some days, weeks or even months and then takes another drink, the vicious circle starts all over again.

The person has a period of wanting to drink, then drinking, followed by stopping and withdrawal symptoms returning. After another few days or weeks, the cycle starts all over again.

Is dependence an illness?

People dependent on alcohol drink in response to triggers – for example, avoiding withdrawal symptoms, or in certain emotional states. The memories of pleasurable feelings from alcohol have been laid down deep in the brain.

This pattern of drinking from habit has been seen in animals studied in scientific laboratories. Some families of animals pass on a genetic tendency to alcohol dependence – so there is strong evidence for the involvement of biological factors.

Someone who is dependent on alcohol has tremendous struggles about whether or not to drink, which most of us never know. But, although there may be a biological basis to this, his or her recovery will depend on how hard an effort is made, as well as how much help is received.

Someone who is dependent on alcohol has tremendous struggles about whether or not to drink, which most of us never know.

KEY POINTS

■ Dependence on alcohol means beginning to 'need' it on some occasions, or repeatedly failing to control the amount

■ Some dependent drinkers get withdrawal symptoms when they cut down or go without

■ There is a chemical basis to dependence on alcohol, but change means wanting to change and making an effort

How to change your drinking pattern

Do I need to cut down?

If you are wondering whether you should change your drinking pattern, weigh up the benefits of drinking against the costs. You can make a list of the pros and cons of your drinking – try to be objective when you do this.

Think about changing your drinking pattern if the disadvantages of drinking outweigh the advantages.

Solution or cause

Is drinking the solution to your problems or the cause? Drinking eats up money and brain cells forever but has never made problems disappear for more than an hour or two.

If you have been using alcohol for tension, you might have begun to think of it as a friend rather than a foe. However, please read pages 45–9 about alcohol and stress, because alcohol can make tension and depression worse.

You may think that your only problem is unfair criticism by your partner or employer. But you may

If you are wondering whether you should change your drinking pattern, weigh up the benefits of drinking against the costs.

have been wearing blinkers – alcohol can definitely blur your memory. Perhaps you have been playing down or not even registering things that you did or said after drinking.

You may be someone who can drink with enjoyment and without any problems usually, but find that just sometimes your drinking goes way over what is safe or right for the occasion. Some people find it very difficult, or impossible, to predict whether, when they have a drink, it will end with trouble.

The pros and cons of drinking

If you are wondering whether you should change your drinking pattern, weigh up the benefits of drinking against the costs. Here is an example to get you thinking.

Advantages
- I enjoy the pub atmosphere
- Helps me to relax
- I feel I talk better after one or two drinks
- It makes me feel less shy with the opposite sex

Disadvantages
- Cost
- Drink is affecting my job
- My family get upset by it
- Sex life isn't so good
- Drinking gives me sickness and stomach pain

Am I at risk of alcoholism?

You may find that the disadvantages of drinking do not at present outweigh the advantages but you want to know if you are at risk. Over 28 units per week for men (21 for women) or regularly drinking over 8 units in a session (5 for women) means that you are likely to run into problems.

Remember, alcoholism runs in families. Take care if your grandparents, uncles, aunts or members of your immediate family have had a drinking problem – you may have inherited some genes that make you more vulnerable (see pages 11–13).

Take action!
Cutting down

If your drinking has begun to cause problems, you will have to make a radical change if you want to be able to carry on drinking but safely. It will mean reducing the days on which you drink, making the maximum amount on any occasion very small, such as three units, so that you do not start dissolving your good intentions with alcohol.

It will probably mean changing the situations where you drink – setting a rule never to drink alone, avoiding certain heavy drinking friends and settings.

If your drinking has begun to cause problems, you will have to make a radical change if you want to be able to carry on drinking but safely.

Stopping

You may know that the best way for you is to keep it simple – to quit. Or maybe you have tried cutting down but failed. Here are some tips on how to succeed.

Remember why

Always keep fresh in your mind why you have decided to quit.

The first few days are the worst

Sweating, tremor, anxiety, 'butterflies in the stomach', not sleeping, nausea and perhaps vomiting, can occur in the first two or three days after stopping drinking. You could avoid this by cutting down gradually over several days, but some people find that hard and prefer to set a date and stop. The urge to have a drink may be strong.

You should stop drinking completely if any of the following circumstances apply

- You exhibit symptoms of dependence for more than a month
- Your partner is not in full agreement with your plan for limited drinking
- You are easily upset or do things on the spur of the moment
- You are not good at sticking to rules – stopping drinking altogether can be easier than reduction and will be simpler for family and friends to understand
- One of your body's organs is damaged
- You have an emotional illness such as depression

Coping with withdrawal symptoms

Very unpleasant symptoms occur only in someone drinking 15 or more units per day (half a bottle of spirits, 5 pints of 3.5 per cent beer). Tranquillisers prescribed by a doctor could be helpful, assuming you are going to stop all alcohol.

Drinking 20–30 units per day (a bottle of spirits or 12 pints of beer) could mean dangerous withdrawal symptoms such as epileptic fits and you must get medical help to reduce the risk (smaller quantities could cause risk in those below average body weight).

Tranquillisers are usually only taken for 4 or 5 days and at most for 10 days. You start with the largest dose in the first 24 hours after your last drink and tail them off until you are taking one tablet or capsule at night on the last night. Do not take alcohol once you have started the course of tranquillisers.

Sleeping

Sleep may be disturbed, but that never harmed anyone. Ways to relax could include taking time off work, having a warm bath at night, listening to favourite music, going for walks or keeping occupied. The sleep pattern gradually returns to normal after about one or two weeks.

Take regular meals

Eat regularly and drink fruit juice or milk. Avoid lots of tea and coffee because caffeine will increase the anxiety of the withdrawal period and prevent sleep, and could increase the urge to drink. Getting hungry can also lead to wanting a drink.

Come clean

It is probably best to tell close friends and relatives that you have stopped drinking and admit that it had been becoming a problem. If you make up a reason such as 'I'm on tablets from the doctor', then in a week or two they will once more be putting pressure on you to have a drink.

Tips to cut down drinking

Maybe you have tried cutting down your drinking in the past and failed. Here are some ideas that might help you to succeed:

- List your reasons for cutting down
- Set rules (realistic ones), for example, 'Saturdays only', 'never alone', 'no more than four units a day'
- Enlist help from family and friends
- Change to a lower strength drink
- Practise saying 'No'
- Sip, don't gulp – pace your drinking
- Avoid heavy drinking friends and buying rounds
- Eat something when drinking
- Don't drink if depressed or angry
- Setback? Figure out why you slipped and how to avoid repeating it. Try again
- If it's not working, try a month or two of not drinking at all to see if that's more successful

Research in specialist clinics has found that the best method to help people become totally abstinent is to link them with Alcoholics Anonymous (AA).

Practise refusing
Practise saying 'No' convincingly, so that you are ready when people offer you a drink.

Keep at it
Complacency is the main reason why people relapse. You will find that, after you have stayed off alcohol for a few weeks, you feel confident that you can now handle it. This may not be true. You may find that quite quickly, even over a few days, your old drinking pattern re-emerges.

Take up a hobby
If drinking took up your time, or was your main hobby, you will need to find a substitute activity. Take up a new interest or one you dropped some years ago. Getting physically fit is a hobby with extra pay-offs!

First drink
Staying away from that first drink is the key to success.

Getting extra help
Medical treatment
Discussion and advice

Your doctor's main role will be to answer questions that you have about drinking and your health, to help you work out the pros and cons of your drinking and, if you decide to make a change, to help you make a plan of action.

Medication for withdrawal symptoms

If you have decided to stop drinking, your doctor can assess whether you need a prescription to control withdrawal symptoms.

He or she may suggest a tranquilliser, probably diazepam or chlordiazepoxide. The largest dose is for the first 24 hours after the last drink, followed by a stepwise reduction over the next 3 to 5 days.

Tranquillisers should not be continued for longer than two weeks, because dependence develops and another vicious circle can be started, where the person feels a strong need for the tablets and gets anxious without them.

Vitamins

Your doctor may prescribe vitamin tablets for you – or you can buy them from your pharmacist. Vitamin B_1, thiamine, is the most important vitamin for a drinker.

Your doctor's main role will be to answer questions that you have about drinking and your health, to help you work out the pros and cons of your drinking and, if you decide to make a change, to help you make a plan of action.

In hospital, the vitamins may be given by injection, which ensures that the vitamins quickly get to the brain cells where they are needed.

Deterrent tablets

Some substances react with alcohol to give a very unpleasant reaction. For example, if you eat the mushroom, inky nightcap, and then drink alcohol, your face goes red and your head and heart pound. Disulfiram (Antabuse) is a medication that acts in the same way.

If you have been taking disulfiram regularly, in a sufficient dose, and then take even small amounts of alcohol, within about 15 minutes your face goes red, your head and heart pound, your breathing feels tight and you may vomit or faint. It is a very unpleasant feeling and, for someone with heart disease or on drugs for lowering blood pressure, it could even be fatal.

Disulfiram has a long action, once a sufficient starting dose has been taken. An alcohol reaction can occur up to seven days later. The tablets (seven per week) can be taken once a day or spaced out with three one day and two on two other days.

As with many medications, some people may notice side effects. Drowsiness is the most common, and for some people disulfiram is best taken near bedtime.

You could arrange with someone to remind you to take it. Otherwise you may 'forget' to take your tablets if you still partly want to drink. You can give confidence to your partner or your employer by letting them see you take your tablet – in which case you should dissolve it in water so that you are not tempted to put it under your tongue and spit it out later! This is called the 'partnership approach'.

Using deterrent tablets is not a sign of weakness. It is a strength to recognise that will-power is not always there when you need it most. The choice to drink or not to drink is still yours – and you make it each time you take a tablet.

If you find this method works for you, keep it up for 6 to 12 months. This gives you time to see that life without alcohol is possible and weakens some of your old habits and triggers to drinking.

Acamprosate

Brain chemistry is altered in people who are dependent on alcohol. When the person becomes abstinent, some of these changes recover in the coming weeks. The sleep pattern gradually returns to normal after a month or so. The person may feel nervous – easily startled by a loud noise, for example. These lingering changes in certain brain pathways leave the person prone to relapse. Relapse into heavy drinking after 'drying out' is common even in people who feel confident and determined.

People who take acamprosate (Campral) tablets in the first six to twelve months after drying out improve their chances of staying clear of alcohol. It must be taken regularly. For reasons that are not understood, it is not effective in some people.

If a drinking slip occurs when people are taking acamprosate, there is no reaction, but they must keep taking the medication and try hard to resume abstinence.

Some people experience diarrhoea in the first two to three days, but usually this is temporary.

Acamprosate is not a tranquilliser and is not addictive. People who take it for a year to help them abstain from alcohol can stop it without withdrawal symptoms or sudden relapse into drinking. It has been thoroughly tested and is very safe. It is an aid, not a magic cure; the person trying to stop drinking who wants to use acamprosate will still have to think about making changes in their approach to life and perhaps in their relationships.

Naltrexone

Naltrexone is a once-a-day tablet that reduces the likelihood of relapse to heavy drinking. It has mainly been tested in people who were aiming to abstain from alcohol. It has been used in North America since 1995 and in many other countries. It is not licensed in the UK for treating alcoholism, but some specialist clinics offer it.

Once again, it is not a magic cure – planning how to handle drinking situations and the emotions that in the past have led to drinking will still be necessary.

Naltrexone interrupts some of the 'endorphin' pathways in the brain. Endorphins have been connected to the experience of pleasure, and have sometimes been called 'natural heroin', but there is no evidence that it blocks general feelings of pleasure or enjoyment in alcohol-dependent patients. However, alcohol-dependent people who have had a drinking slip when taking naltrexone report that they find it easier to put the brakes on. It can reduce the chance that drinking will spiral out of control. It may also interrupt some of the triggers to drinking, and patients taking it report that they think less about alcohol and the pleasures of drinking. Some patients take it daily, and others take it only on days when they plan to have one or two drinks or predict that they might be in a situation where they might drink. It is important that it is in the body for at least an hour before that first drink.

In animals, interest in drinking alcohol gradually diminishes when naltrexone is given before consuming alcohol. Sometimes we see this in patients, but so far there is no scientific study showing that it can permanently extinguish the attraction to alcohol in people who have been alcohol dependent.

Naltrexone causes nausea in about one person in ten, which usually passes after the first few days. Headache or sleep disturbance occurs in a few. It is not a tranquilliser and is not addictive. Some people have safely taken naltrexone for several years because they feel that it has helped them avoid relapse to alcoholic drinking.

Baclofen

In 2008, news spread that a medicine in use for many years to treat muscle spasm, baclofen, might be a safe aid to people dependent an alcohol who were trying to abstain. As with naltrexone and acamprosate, brain chemistry studies had identified a potential place where a medicine such as baclofen might impact on the addictive cycle of dependent drinkers. Researchers found that patients with liver or other physical damage from alcohol who were prescribed baclofen three times per day could be helped to abstain and experience less craving for alcohol in the coming weeks after leaving hospital. Reports of individuals who did not have liver disease were also published, describing dramatic benefits attributed to using very large doses of baclofen. Often these were people who had used alcohol to relieve anxiety.

Baclofen is not licensed in any country for this use. However, specialists are prescribing it with reports of success in people who had failed to abstain using other medications, AA and traditional therapies.

When first taken, baclofen causes slight sedation in most people, and so it is prescribed in a low dose and very gradually increased over the coming three to four weeks. Baclofen seems to be a safe medicine, because there are thousands of patients worldwide who have taken it, sometimes for many years, to treat muscle spasm, and there are few reports of unwanted effects. However, it is too early to be certain about its safety in treating people dependent on alcohol, especially when used in larger doses.

Help for anxiety and fears

Some anxious people find that they gradually become calmer after they stop drinking and do not need further help. If anxiety or panicky feelings continue, finding ways to relax and control anxiety or overcome fears by facing the feared situation (called exposure therapy) can be all that is needed.

Tranquillisers such as diazepam are best avoided because you can become dependent on them. Drugs used for depression can help anxiety, panic attacks and some phobias. These are not drugs that people abuse and can be safely used for months or even years, but they should be reduced and stopped only very gradually because there can be 'withdrawal' effects.

Treatment for depressive illness

You may need this if you experience a low, hopeless or worried feeling, which goes on for weeks and cannot be linked to anything particular going wrong. This is not the low or fed-up feeling that we have when we

Some anxious people find that they gradually become calmer after they stop drinking.

have had a bad day – unless we plan to wallow in it, we are probably OK by next morning.

In depressive illness, sufferers lose the ability to experience fun and joy, are caught up in pessimistic thoughts, irritable and easily tired, and may feel undue guilt. They may even feel so worthless and hopeless that they have thoughts of suicide.

They tend to wake in the small hours and lie awake worrying. Their appetite may decrease and they may lose interest in sex. Alcohol is a very bad treatment for depression. Avoid it completely, or at most have one drink (half a pint of beer or one glass of wine) only very occasionally.

There is a good chance of full recovery from depressive illness. Psychotherapy – talking therapy – with a counsellor, doctor or psychologist will help you keep your thoughts in perspective and prevent them spiralling downwards. The therapy will help you regain a belief in your own qualities and not let comments by others or feelings of resentment fester and cause inner anger.

The chemical changes in your brain that go with depression can be corrected by getting your thoughts in order and getting more enjoyment from relationships and your life. In addition, antidepressants can help to correct these changes.

They can be used for several months – or even for years by people who tend to have relapses of the illness and therefore need a preventive strategy. Side effects vary depending on the type of tablet prescribed, and are only common in the first three to four days.

Some types have a sedative effect that can immediately help sleep but could interfere with driving. Other types can cause nausea or anxiety in the first few days, although this usually passes.

Antidepressants take three to six weeks to have their main effect, so it is important to give them a fair chance to work.

Specialist centres

There are National Health Service and private clinics offering treatment for alcohol dependence. Private clinics tend to be residential and may be costly, whereas in the NHS you are usually seen and treated as an outpatient.

In Britain it is usual to make contact with specialist clinics through your GP but you do not have to do this if you strongly prefer to refer yourself direct, perhaps because you fear (possibly quite unreasonably) your GP's reaction.

The clinics use group therapy to overcome shame and secrecy – you meet others with whom you can identify. It helps you to see things in a broader perspective, as well as to get tips on how to handle life without alcohol.

People gain in strength and confidence with group therapy. This can help with the social anxiety that some drinkers have struggled with – boosting self-confidence and teaching how to be constructively assertive.

The clinic will probably want to have contact with your family too. It is important to have your family's views on what has been happening and what help is needed and the clinic may have useful advice for them.

Counselling

Many cities have 'alcohol advice centres' or 'councils on alcohol' giving individual guidance and support. The counsellors are trained, lay volunteers. These centres are listed in your local telephone directory.

Alcoholics Anonymous

AA is a fellowship of men and women who have an honest desire to stop drinking. They have recognised that they are 'powerless over alcohol'. Experience has shown them that by meeting together and living by simple, sensible guidelines – such as 'take life one day at a time' – they can stay away from the first drink.

What are meetings like?

The atmosphere is warm and welcoming. Some repetitiveness at the meetings is deliberate. People who have had a drink problem know how easy it is to forget the problems that alcohol caused. When they forget, the next relapse is one step nearer. At AA people keep the memory of those problems fresh in their minds, resisting the temptation that we all have to gloss over past pain.

Is it religious?

There is a 'spiritual' element to AA. Although you may hear people talking about god or a higher power at AA, there are many atheists who have found that AA has helped them enormously. There are AA groups in most countries of the world and it is not linked to any church or religion.

How can it help?

Meeting members of AA can give hope to you if you are still in the midst of your problem and fear that it is insuperable. There are some people who will never overcome their drink problem unless they draw regularly on the strength and companionship to be found at AA.

The contact for your local AA group is listed in your local telephone directory.

Research in specialist clinics has found that the best method to get people totally abstinent is to link them with AA.

Help on the internet

There is also help on the internet (see 'Useful addresses', page 106). The AA website will give you information about how it helps people. A newer self-help group for people with alcohol problems is SMART.

SMART (Self Management and Recovery Training) is well established in North America. It has an active web page, with chat lines and support options. Read about its humanistic philosophy, in which drinking is seen as choice.

Smart Recovery teaches that negative thinking can lead us into fairly unproductive choices at times! But we can be smart and re-train some old thought patterns.

KEY POINTS

- Some who develop alcohol problems can't successfully cut down. If that's not working, get help to quit completely

- Try Alcoholics Anonymous – it's a very successful method

- If you're determined but still cannot stick to it, consider deterrent tablets or the anti-craving medicines

- Keep the whole family in the picture

Advice for family, friends and colleagues

Don't cover up

Family and friends, colleagues and supervisors typically try to shield someone with a drink problem, at least initially. They make excuses and cover up, believing that the drinker will soon realise what is happening and do something to put it right.

The drinking may, however, become more fixed as dependence intensifies. Praying for a miracle to happen is not usually the answer. Sympathy on its own may achieve nothing – or even enable more drinking. Unless drinkers face the consequences of how alcohol affects them, they just go on repeating the same mistakes.

It can be helpful and constructive to say something to get the drinker to take stock, but sensitivity is necessary. Remember that the drinker has many positive qualities and that the subject of complaint is only the drinking and the behaviour it brings. There is no need to write off the whole person.

Family and friends, colleagues and supervisors typically try to shield someone with a drink problem, at least initially.

Control may be counterproductive

If someone is determined to drink, there is little anyone can do until there is a change of mind. To try to control the situation can be exhausting and frustrating – although you should intervene if there is danger of harm to others – for example, drinking and driving. However, when you let go of your efforts to control, you not only save your energy, you also remove one of the drinker's excuses for drinking. He or she cannot blame you for the drinking because you are nagging or bossy. But don't stop giving a firm message that you insist on some change.

Getting things out in the open

Drinkers may fool themselves about the quantity that they drink and its harmful consequences. This is partly because they cannot always remember what they did when they drank a lot. It is also because if they admit there is a problem then it would be logical to give up some drinking.

If they still enjoy it or feel they need it, then that would be a painful conclusion to reach. This is what is meant by denial.

Dealing with denial

The more head-on the confrontation, the more denial there can be. It is better to start a discussion with open-ended questions such as 'How are you feeling these days?' or 'What are your concerns at present?' leading to 'How do you think your drinking might fit into the picture?'.

If someone is determined to drink, there is little anyone can do until there is a change of mind.

Choose your timing. Do not expect to be able to talk usefully if tempers are raised or the brain is clouded by drink. The 'morning after' may be a good time – or when there has been a crisis.

Set clear limits
Let the drinker know what you can and cannot tolerate. Be ready to admit where you have gone wrong and accept criticism if it is justified, but do not take any blame for the drinking. That is entirely the responsibility of the drinker.

Idle threats, or threats that you cannot follow through, are pointless. At work, sanctions should be put in writing. At home, make it clear what your needs are and be prepared to negotiate – not about the drinking, but about other ways in which life could be improved by changes on both sides.

If there's no change
In a family, life has to go on and you and your children have to survive. There are different ways in which you can get outside help (see pages 75–87).

Keeping the emotional temperature down may help prevent the family from doing things that they would later regret. Sometimes couples separate if a drinker cannot or will not take steps to cut back.

Help for the family
Counselling agencies often provide support and advice for partners as well as the drinker and there are self-help groups.

Al-Anon is a wonderful self-help fellowship for families and friends of those with drinking problems and Alateen is for teenage sons and daughters. The contacts of local groups can be found in your local telephone directory (see pages 106–7).

Living with someone with a drink problem can be taxing and depressing. There is a limit to what we can do if our partner, friend or relative wants to drink and is dependent on alcohol.

Al-Anon helps you keep yourself strong and well, and stops you getting eaten up with guilt, anger or frustration. The message is 'detach with love' rather than exhaust yourself struggling with someone else's addiction.

You will get no advice on how to track down the hidden alcohol supplies or catch out the secret drinker in his or her lair – but you may find yourself feeling calmer and less consumed with tension and resentments!

Sometimes couples separate if a drinker cannot or will not take steps to cut back.

KEY POINTS

■ A drink problem doesn't mean writing off the whole person

■ The family should give a clear message

■ The drinker is the only one responsible for the drinking, but others should accept criticism if it is justified

Children, teenagers and parents

Children, alcohol and the law

Under the Licensing Act of 1902, it is an offence to be drunk in charge of a child under the age of seven on any highway, public house, licensed premises, public place, building or inn.

The Children's Act of 1908 banned the use of alcohol by any child under the age of five except for medicinal purposes, and banned children under the age of 14 from the bar of a licensed premise. The Licensing Act of 1964 stated that no one under the age of 18 can be employed in a bar.

At 14, a child can be taken into a bar, but must not consume alcohol. At 16 he or she can buy and drink wine, beer or cider in a restaurant. No intoxicating liquor can be sold or delivered to a person under 18 years of age.

It has been suggested that for newly qualified drivers age 18 to 20 – the age when road accidents are most common – the legal limit for drinking and driving should be lower than 80 mg% or even zero. However, it is good to see that many young people nowadays have a rule about not drinking any alcohol if they are driving.

Alcohol can be an attraction to teenagers that can lead them into trouble.

Clubs, pubs, parties and teenagers

Going out for a drink is as much part of life for teenagers as it is for adults – perhaps even more, because being with your friends seems to be essential at that age. The popular meeting places often depend on the profits from serving alcohol, including student unions at college and university.

Some young people overdo it from early on in their drinking days. Some will run into difficulties by drinking and driving, having an accident or falling out with friends. Some will start drinking to solve a problem – a habit that over the coming months or years could lead to major problems. That applies if it is drinking to help shyness or drinking because of being fed-up or bored.

Let your friends, parents or a school counsellor help if you have worries. There may be another way round the problem. You may just need to be told that being the quiet, shy person in your group of friends is OK – no one wants you to be incredibly talkative or witty anyhow!

Saying 'No' can be hard if you are already self-conscious about how you fit in with your group. However, keeping your head and not giving way to pressure shows you have personality. You have the right to say 'No'.

Some young people overdo it from early on in their drinking days.

Advice to parents

- Introduce sensible drinking at home if your teenagers say they would like a drink.

- Advise eating something, even some crisps or chips, if they are out drinking with their friends, to help them avoid getting drunk.

- No drinking when driving, cycling or swimming.

- Let them know what the law is on drinking – for example, the minimum age for buying alcohol in a bar, off-licence or supermarket is 18.

- Is your own drinking pattern setting an example that you would like them to copy? Our children tend to follow what they see us do more than what we tell them to do!

- Be a good listener – check that the communication channel is working!

KEY POINTS

- Young people with worries should get help by talking to someone

- Children tend to follow what their parents do, not what they say

Drinking, driving, working and the law

Drinking and driving

One-quarter of all road traffic fatalities have blood alcohol levels over the legal limit. This increases to 60 per cent for deaths occurring between 10pm and 4am. The greatest number of such fatalities are in the 20–24 year age group. Random roadside tests by the Department of Transport reveal that 17 per cent of people driving between 10pm and 3am are over the limit.

Legal limit

The law in Britain states that you must not drive, or be in charge of a car, if you are unfit to drive, or have more than 80 milligrams of alcohol in 100 millilitres of blood (80 mg%). This is the same as 0.35 milligram in 1 litre of breath.

This level of alcohol in your blood is reached after drinking four to five units of alcohol in one or two hours. Or you could have that level in your bloodstream several hours after your last drink, or even the next day, if you had drunk a lot.

But people vary and drinking the same amount of alcohol will give different levels in different people. A higher level is reached if you are small or if you are drinking on an empty stomach.

Providing a specimen

It is also an offence to fail to provide a specimen for analysis while attempting to drive. Conviction for driving over the limit means a fine, a ban from driving for at least a year and higher insurance premiums.

If your blood alcohol level is two and a half times above the legal limit, or if it is a second offence in 10 years, or if you refuse to give a breath or blood sample, then before your licence is returned after the ban you have to pass a medical examination to check that you do not still have a drinking problem. This is called the 'High Risk Offender Scheme'.

What if I'm below the limit?

Driving is impaired well below the legal limit of 80 mg%. Even after two units (one pint of beer or two glasses of wine), giving a blood alcohol level of around 30 mg%, many drivers have slower reactions and make errors at the wheel. Apart from the personal consequences consider the tragedy you can inflict on others.

DVLA

When we apply for a driving licence, or renew a licence, we are required to tell the DVLA (Driver and Vehicle Licensing Agency) if we have any of a list of medical conditions that could affect driving, such as epilepsy, heart disease, etc. Included in this list is 'alcohol dependence' and 'persistent misuse of alcohol'.

It is up to us to tell the DVLA if we develop any of these conditions. It would be rare for a doctor to inform the DVLA directly about a patient and extremely unusual to do so without informing the patient.

Alcohol dependence or misuse would most certainly prevent you being given a licence for large goods vehicles or passenger-carrying vehicles until you could show that you were clear of the problem for three years.

An ordinary licence might be allowed, if a medical examination with blood tests showed that you had overcome the problem. The DVLA might ask for you to have a medical check-up after another year.

Drinking and work
Comments and warnings

In most work places, it is a breach of discipline to be under the influence of alcohol at work. This would lead to a warning, either verbal or written. If performance was impaired by the hangover effects of drinking, this could lead to comment.

Being frequently absent from work might be another cause for a warning. The manager might also notice a pattern, such as frequent Monday absences or (if pay day is Thursday!) frequent Friday absences.

Not only is it likely to be a breach of your employment contract to be under the influence of alcohol, but it may also be very dangerous.

Frequent time off for vague complaints – gastritis, flu, 'nervous tension', 'stress' – is also more common in a worker who is developing a drinking problem.

Workplace policy

Many employers have a policy for staff who may have a drinking problem. The object is to encourage recovery as soon as possible, while protecting the workplace and other employees from danger. They may not want to dismiss a highly trained colleague who, when sober, is a very good worker.

It is usually easier to recover from a drink problem if you are still in work, so it is good that some managers pick up a problem in an employee at an early stage and take steps before dismissal is necessary. Otherwise managers and colleagues may say nothing, hoping the drinker will see the obvious and do something about it.

If the problem goes on, praying for a miracle is less effective than saying something direct to the person. It is better not to keep on covering up, doing the job for him or her, or making excuses. The sooner someone brings the problem into the open the better.

If there has been a disciplinary issue, the employer may require the employee to seek advice or be examined by the occupational health physician of the company.

The employee who chooses to follow this route may be expected to seek outside help and agree to the helping agency (counselling service or clinic) giving a report on progress to the employer. The report would not normally give any personal details, but states whether or not the individual is attending appointments and following advice.

KEY POINTS

- Even below the legal alcohol limit, driving can still be erratic after drinking

- A drink–drive offence means a ban, a fine and higher insurance

- If an employee's drinking affects work, it is better to bring it up than to cover it up

Useful addresses

We have included the following organisations because, on preliminary investigation, they may be of use to the reader. However, we do not have first-hand experience of each organisation and so cannot guarantee the organisation's integrity. The reader must therefore exercise his or her own discretion and judgement when making further enquiries.

Al-Anon Family Groups UK and Eire (also Alateen)
61 Great Dover Street
London SE1 4YF
Helpline: 020 7403 0888 (24 hours a day)
Website: www.al-anonuk.org.uk

Offers support to families and friends of problem drinkers; can refer to local groups. Alateen, part of Al-Anon, is dedicated to helping teenagers with an alcoholic relative. For details of local meetings ring the helpline.

Al-Anon Information Centre
Republic of Ireland
Room 5, 5 Capel Street

Dublin 1, Republic of Ireland
Helpline: 01 873 2699 (10.30am–2.30pm, Mon–Fri)

Northern Ireland
Peace House, 224 Lisburn Road
Belfast BT9 6GE
Helpline: 028 9068 2368 (Mon–Fri 10am–1pm,
6–11pm, 7 days a week)

Scotland
Mansfield Park Building, Unit 6, 22 Mansfield Street
Partick, Glasgow G11 5QP
Helpline: 0141 339 8884 (10am–10pm, 365 days a year)

Alcohol Concern
64 Leman Street
London E1 8EU
Tel: 020 7264 0510
Website: www.alcoholconcern.org.uk

Agency working against alcohol misuse at national as
well as local level. Supports specialist and non-specialist
service providers helping to tackle all problems at a
local level. Members receive regular magazine and
have access to information and training services.

Alcohol Concern Cymrn
Sophia House, 28 Cathedral Road
Cardiff CF11 9LJ
Tel: 029 2066 0248
Website: www.alcoholconcern.org.uk

See above for information.

Alcohol Education and Research Council (AERC)

Eliot House (EH 1.4), 10–12 Allington Street
London SW1E 5EH
Tel: 020 7808 7150
Website: www.aerc.org.uk

Funds alcohol research and innovative educational projects in the UK. Information on completed projects can be found on the website, especially via the Alcohol Insights series.

Alcohol Focus Scotland

166 Buchanan Street
Glasgow G1 2LW
Tel: 0141 572 6700
Website: www.alcohol-focus-scotland.org.uk

Offers information and support services including public health and campaigns on issues related to alcohol problems. Also provides training to volunteers staffing helpline.

Alcoholics Anonymous (AA)

PO Box 1, 10 Toft Green
York YO1 7NJ
Tel: 01904 644 026
Helpline: 0845 769 7555
Website: www.alcoholics-anonymous.org.uk

Offers information and support, via local groups, to people with alcohol problems who want to stop drinking.

Benefits Enquiry Line

Tel: 0800 882200
Minicom: 0800 243355
Website: www.dwp.gov.uk
N. Ireland: 0800 220674

Government agency giving information and advice on sickness and disability benefits for people with disabilities and their carers.

Citizens Advice Bureaux

Myddleton House, 115–123 Pentonville Road
London N1 9LZ
Website: www.adviceguide.org.uk

HQ of national charity offering a wide variety of practical, financial and legal advice. Network of local charities throughout the UK listed in phone books and in *Yellow Pages* under 'C'.

Clinical Knowledge Summaries

Sowerby Centre for Health Informatics at Newcastle (SCHIN Ltd)
Bede House, All Saints Business Centre
Newcastle upon Tyne NE1 2ES
Tel: 0191 243 6100
Website: www.cks.library.nhs.uk

A website mainly for GPs giving information for patients listed by disease plus named self-help organisations.

Drinkline

Helpline: 0800 917 8282 (24 hours a day, 7 days a week)

Department of Health confidential helpline offering information and advice to callers who are concerned about their own or someone else's drinking. Can refer to local support services.

National Institute for Health and Clinical Excellence (NICE)

MidCity Place, 71 High Holborn
London WC1V 6NA
Tel: 0845 003 7780
Website: www.nice.org.uk

Provides national guidance on the promotion of good health and treatment of ill-health. Patient information leaflets are available for each piece of guidance issued.

NHS Direct

Tel: 0845 4647 (24 hours, 365 days a year)
Website: www.nhsdirect.nhs.uk

Offers confidential health-care advice, information and referral service. A good first port of call for any health advice.

NHS Smoking Helpline

Freephone: 0800 022 4332 (7am–11pm, 365 days a year)
Website: http://smokefree.nhs.uk
Pregnancy smoking helpline: 0800 169 9169
(12 noon–9pm, 365 days a year)

Have advice, help and encouragement on giving up smoking. Specialist advisers available to offer ongoing support to those who genuinely are trying to give up smoking. Can refer to local branches.

Patients' Association

PO Box 935
Harrow, Middlesex HA1 3YJ
Helpline: 0845 608 4455
Tel: 020 8423 9111
Website: www.patients-association.com

Provides advice on patients' rights, leaflets and a
directory of self-help groups.

Quit (Smoking Quitlines)

63 St Mary's Axe
London EC3 8AA
Helpline: 0800 002200 (9am–9pm, 365 days a year)
Tel: 020 7469 0400
Website: www.quit.org.uk

Offers individual advice on giving up smoking in
English and Asian languages. Talks to schools on
smoking and pregnancy and can refer to local support
groups. Runs training courses for professionals.

Useful links

BBC

www.bbc.co.uk/health

A helpful website: easy to navigate and offers lots of
useful advice and information. Also contains links to
other related topics.

Patient UK

www.patient.co.uk

Patient care website.

US Government

www.niaaa.nih.gov

The internet as a further source of information

After reading this book, you may feel that you would like further information on the subject. The internet is of course an excellent place to look and there are many websites with useful information about medical disorders, related charities and support groups.

For those who do not have a computer at home some bars and cafes offer facilities for accessing the internet. These are listed in the Yellow Pages under 'Internet Bars and Cafes' and 'Internet Providers'. Your local library offers a similar facility and has staff to help you find the information that you need.

It should always be remembered, however, that the internet is unregulated and anyone is free to set up a website and add information to it. Many websites offer impartial advice and information that has been compiled and checked by qualified medical professionals. Some, on the other hand, are run by commercial organisations with the purpose of promoting their own products. Others still are run by pressure groups, some of which will provide carefully assessed and accurate information whereas others may be suggesting medications or treatments that are not supported by the medical and scientific community.

Unless you know the address of the website you want to visit – for example, www.familydoctor.co.uk – you may find the following guidelines useful when searching the internet for information.

Search engines and other searchable sites

Google (www.google.co.uk) is the most popular search engine used in the UK, followed by Yahoo! (http://uk.yahoo.com) and MSN (www.msn.co.uk). Also popular are the search engines provided by Internet Service Providers such as Tiscali and other sites such as the BBC site (www.bbc.co.uk).

In addition to the search engines that index the whole web, there are also medical sites with search facilities, which act almost like mini-search engines, but cover only medical topics or even a particular area of medicine. Again, it is wise to look at who is responsible for compiling the information offered to ensure that it is impartial and medically accurate. The NHS Direct site (www.nhsdirect.nhs.uk) is an example of a searchable medical site.

Links to many British medical charities can be found at the Association of Medical Research Charities' website (www.amrc.org.uk) and at Charity Choice (www.charitychoice.co.uk).

Search phrases

Be specific when entering a search phrase. Searching for information on 'cancer' will return results for many different types of cancer as well as on cancer in general. You may even find sites offering astrological information. More useful results will be returned by using search phrases such as 'lung cancer' and 'treatments for lung cancer'. Both Google and Yahoo! offer an advanced search option that includes the ability to search for the exact phrase, enclosing the search phrase in quotes, that is, 'treatments for lung cancer' will have the same effect. Limiting a search to an exact phrase reduces the number of results returned but it is best to refine a search to an exact match only if you are not getting useful results with a normal search. Adding 'UK' to your search term will bring up mainly British sites, so a good phrase might be 'lung cancer' UK (don't include UK within the quotes).

Always remember the internet is international and unregulated. It holds a wealth of valuable information but individual sites may be biased, out of date or just plain wrong. Family Doctor Publications accepts no responsibility for the content of links published in this series.

Index

Your pages

We have included the following pages because they may help you manage your illness or condition and its treatment.

Before an appointment with a health professional, it can be useful to write down a short list of questions of things that you do not understand, so that you can make sure that you do not forget anything.

Some of the sections may not be relevant to your circumstances.

We are always pleased to receive constructive criticism or suggestions about how to improve the books. You can contact us at:

Email: familydoctor@btinternet.com
Letter: Family Doctor Publications
         PO Box 4664
         Poole
         BH15 1NN

Thank you

Health-care contact details

Name:

Job title:

Place of work:

Tel:

Name:

Job title:

Place of work:

Tel:

Name:

Job title:

Place of work:

Tel:

Name:

Job title:

Place of work:

Tel:

Significant past health events – illnesses/operations/investigations/treatments

Event	Month	Year	Age (at time)

Appointments for health care

Name:

Place:

Date:

Time:

Tel:

Name:

Place:

Date:

Time:

Tel:

Name:

Place:

Date:

Time:

Tel:

Name:

Place:

Date:

Time:

Tel:

Appointments for health care

Name:

Place:

Date:

Time:

Tel:

Name:

Place:

Date:

Time:

Tel:

Name:

Place:

Date:

Time:

Tel:

Name:

Place:

Date:

Time:

Tel:

Current medication(s) prescribed by your doctor

Medicine name:

Purpose:

Frequency & dose:

Start date:

End date:

Medicine name:

Purpose:

Frequency & dose:

Start date:

End date:

Medicine name:

Purpose:

Frequency & dose:

Start date:

End date:

Medicine name:

Purpose:

Frequency & dose:

Start date:

End date:

Other medicines/supplements you are taking, not prescribed by your doctor

Medicine/treatment:

Purpose:

Frequency & dose:

Start date:

End date:

Medicine/treatment:

Purpose:

Frequency & dose:

Start date:

End date:

Medicine/treatment:

Purpose:

Frequency & dose:

Start date:

End date:

Medicine/treatment:

Purpose:

Frequency & dose:

Start date:

End date:

Questions to ask at appointments
(Note: do bear in mind that doctors work under great time pressure, so long lists may not be helpful for either of you)